Supporting Literacy

FOR AGES 5–6

Introduction

Supporting Literacy is aimed at all those who work with children who have been identified as needing 'additional' or 'different' literacy support. It can be used by anyone working with children who fall into this category, whether you are a teacher, classroom assistant or parent.

Typically the five to six year-old children for whom the book is intended will be working at the levels expected of Pre-school or Reception children or may simply need extra help in tackling the standard of work expected of Year 1. Their difficulties may be short term, and overcome with extra practice and support on a one to one or small group basis, or they may be long term where such support enables them to make progress but at a level behind their peer group. The activities in this book provide exactly what these children need – plenty of repetition and practice of basic skills, often covering the same ground but in a slightly different way. For this reason, you might decide to use the worksheets in a different order or just select the sheets that are suitable for the child or group of children you are working with. All the activities can be used on their own or alongside other literacy schemes that are already established within your school.

The worksheets are simple and self-explanatory and the instruction text is deliberately kept to a minimum to make the pages easy for adults to use and less daunting for children to follow. At the bottom of each page 'Notes for teachers' summarise the purpose of the activity and the learning target that is being addressed. Suggestions for additional activities are included if appropriate.

Most of the worksheets are based upon the National Literacy Strategy (NLS) objectives but some, where possible and relevant, are linked to other aspects of the curriculum. Through many years of experience of working with special needs children, the authors have been able to select the areas that these children find most difficult and provide useful activities that specifically address these stumbling blocks. Accordingly, and as set out below, most of the worksheets are centred around the word level strand of the Literacy Strategy.

The main targets addressed in this book are:
- Learning to read the NLS high frequency Reception words
- Learning the letters of the alphabet and the sounds they make
- Learning and identifying initial sounds in words
- Sounding out cvc words (all vowels are included as medial sound, eg, bag, bet, bit, pot, run)
- Learning the blends ch, sh, th
- Using picture clues to help decode text
- Recognising rhyming words
- Correcting b/d confusion
- Sequencing a set of 4 pictures
- Sequencing a set of sentences

However you decide to use these sheets and in whatever context, it is worth remembering that children generally achieve the greatest success in an atmosphere of support and encouragement. Praise from a caring adult can be the best reward for children's efforts. The worksheets and activities in this book will provide many opportunities for children to enjoy their successes. The resulting increase in self-esteem will make a difference to their school work and other areas of school life too.

Individual record sheet

Name:

Worksheet	Teaching and learning objective			Target achieved	Needs more practice
	NLS sight words (new)	NLS sight words (revised)	Other context words introduced		
1-2	a can cat dog I see				
3-4	is mum my this	can cat dog I see			
5-6	and like me school they you	I my			
7-8	going he she the to was	mum is see	clown		
9-10	away come go play went	and I dog the to you			
11-12	am are in	cat dog he I is she the you	tractor		
13-14	Dad no said yes	can I see the they you	owl		
15-16	big it	a dad is mum school the	horse		
17-18	all look up we you	I they	down		
19-20	at on	cat dog in the	house roof		
21-22	get	a I in is mum on the	bus		
23-24	Day for	a am go going on I the they we	train out		
25-26	of	can get I is the they	here boat off		
27	To learn the letters of the alphabet in order				
28	To correct b/d confusion				
29	To identify the initial letter sound 'p'				
30	To identify the initial letter sound 'm'				
31	To identify the initial letter sound 'b'				
32	To identify the final sound 'd' in consonant-vowel-consonant (cvc) words				
33	To identify the final sound 'g' in (cvc) words				
34	To identify the final sound 'n' in (cvc) words				
35	To identify rhyme and to find words that rhyme with cat/hat and dog/frog				
36	To identify rhyme and to find words that rhyme with cat/bat/flat and pig/wig				
37	To identify rhyme and to find words that rhyme with play/day and sad/lad				
38	To read words with initial sounds: ch, sh, th				
39	To read words with initial sound 'ch'				
40	To read words with initial sound 'sh'				
41	To read words with initial sound 'th'				
42	To sequence a set of four pictures identifying what each picture shows				
43	To sequence a set of four sentences to match the corresponding pictures				
44	To sequence a set of four pictures identifying what each picture shows				
45	To sequence a set of four sentences to match the corresponding pictures				
46	To sequence a set of four pictures identifying what each picture shows				
47	To sequence a set of four sentences to match the corresponding pictures				
48	To sequence a set of four pictures identifying what each picture shows				
49	To sequence a set of four sentences to match the corresponding pictures				

Record and Review

Name: _____   Date of birth: _____

Teacher: _____   Class: _____

Support assistant: _____

Code of Practice stage: _____   Date targets set: _____

Target

1 _____

2 _____

3 _____

4 _____

Review

Target

1 _____

_____

_____ Target achieved? ☐ Date: _____

2 _____

_____

_____ Target achieved? ☐ Date: _____

3 _____

_____

_____ Target achieved? ☐ Date: _____

4 _____

_____

_____ Target achieved? ☐ Date: _____

Content of the worksheets

Worksheets 1–26 The first twenty-six worksheets concentrate specifically on the target of learning the 45 high frequency words that are identified in List 1 of the NLS to be achieved by the end of Reception. It recommends that these words are taught as 'sight recognition' words in the Reception Year but many children are stll not familiar with these words when they first come into Year 1.

They are listed here in alphabetical order for ease of reference but we certainly do not recommend that children learn them in this order.

a	all	am	and	are	at	away	big	can	cat	come
dad	day	dog	for	get	go	going	he	I	in	is	it
like	look	me	mum	my	no	of	on	play	said	see
she	the	they	this	to	up	was	we	went	yes	you

It is essential that pupils who are showing signs of delayed progress should be supported with learning these 'sight recognition' words. They are not easy words to learn, particularly as the set contains very few nouns. For this reason our worksheets provide repeated practice of recognising and reading these words. The notes for adults on each sheet indicate how the words can be used in context through the children reading and creating simple phrases or sentences. Each worksheet contains appropriate words for this purpose.

Worksheet 27 is a single sheet designed for the purpose of learning the alphabet as specified in the NLS for Reception and Year 1. Worksheet 28 supports worksheet 27 by providing practice in overcoming b/d confusion, an extremely common stubbling block for many, many children.

Worksheets 29 to 34 feature consonant-vowel-consonant words. We encourage children to look closely at these, sounding out carefully the initial phoneme for each word and the final phoneme for each word, both of which are single consonants. Most consonants require the child to close their lips, to 'bite' the lower lip or to touch the roof of the mouth with the tongue. The exception to the rule is 'h'. The children can also be encouraged to look at the central phoneme for each word. These are, of course, the vowels, a, e, i, o, u. They are 'open' sounds as they are made with the mouth open.

A set of flashcards showing cvc words, together with pictures to which they can be matched, can be created from Resource sheets D, E amd F on pages 59-61.

A larger range of cvc flashcards, to be used with Worksheets 29 to 34, can be made from Resource sheets G, H and I on pages 62-64. Please refer to the Notes for teachers on page 55.

Worksheets 35, 36 and 37 provide opportunities to identify and practise rhyming words, including some words that are more complex than cvc words.

Worksheets 38 to 41 offer support with the blends ch, sh and th.

Worksheets 42 to 49 are designed to support children in the literacy associated with some of the science work that will take place in Year 1 regarding 'Ourselves' and 'Growing'. In completing these worksheets with support, the children will gain valuable experience in sequencing pictures – this provides opportunities for speaking and listening, through the discussions that take place regarding what the pictures show and why they should be arranged in a particular order. Arranging the sentences in order involves reading them repeatedly to gain understanding of their meaning.

If you wish the child could stick the pictures on to a separate piece of paper with the appropriate sentence written underneath each one. Alternatively a simple four-page book could be made with a picture and sentence on each page.

Name: _____ Date: _____

Read the words.

Notes for teachers
Target: To read these YR high frequency NLS words: a, can, cat, dog, I, see
This sheet can be used to record each child's progress. As the child successfully reads each word s/he can colour it on the sheet. You may like to take the opportunity to encourage the child to create a simple phrase or sentence using some of the words on the sheet. Write the child's sentence down so that s/he can copy it. Encourage careful writing and well formed letters.

Name: **Date:**

Read the words.

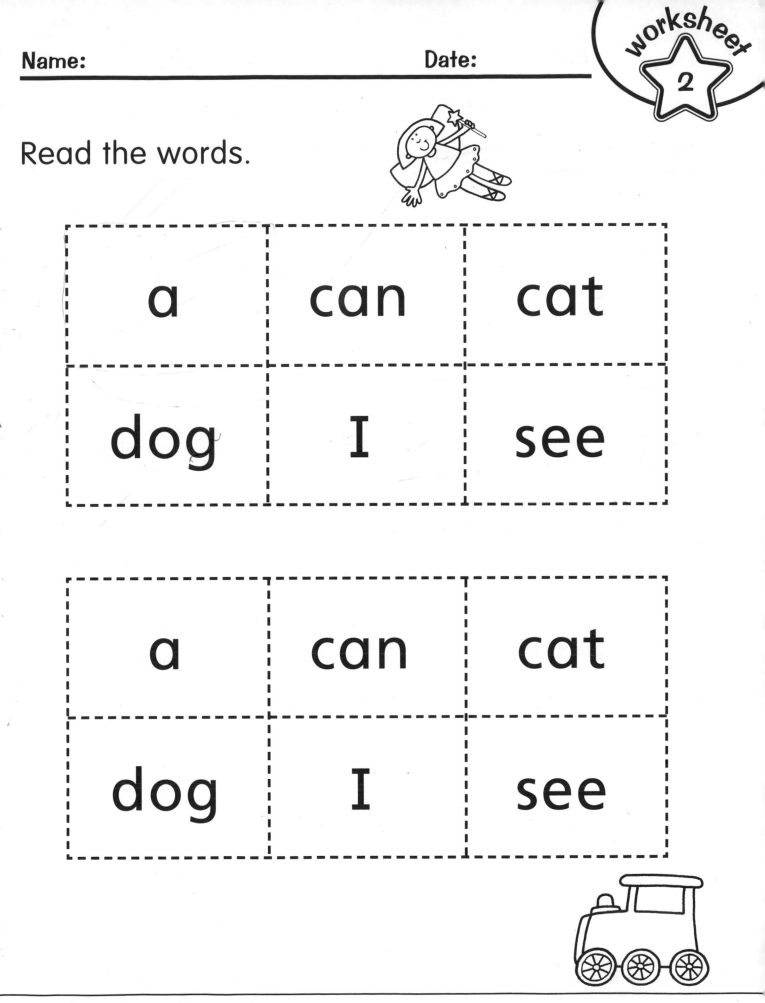

a	can	cat
dog	I	see

a	can	cat
dog	I	see

Notes for teachers

Target: To read these YR high frequency NLS words: a, can, cat, dog, I, see
The children should cut out both sets of words and use them for making pairs, playing snap and matching to the 'castle' words on Worksheet 1. Can the children make any phrases using the word cards? The following are possible: I see a cat. I see a dog. I can see a cat. I can see a dog.

Name: _____   **Date:** _____

Read the words.

is

this

mum

cat

dog

my

Notes for teachers

Target: To read these YR high frequency NLS words: cat, dog, is, mum, my, this

This sheet can be used to record each child's progress. As a child successfully reads each word s/he can colour it on the sheet. You may like to take the opportunity to encourage the child to create a simple phrase or sentence using some of the words on the sheet. Write the child's sentence down so that s/he can copy it. Encourage careful writing and well formed letters.

worksheet
4

Read the words.

cat	dog	is
mum	my	this
cat	dog	is
mum	my	this

Notes for teachers

Target: To read these YR high frequency NLS words: cat, dog, is, mum, my, this

The children should cut out both sets of words and use them for making pairs, playing snap and matching to the 'car' words on worksheet 3. Can the children make any phrases using the word cards? The following are possible: this is my cat, this is my dog, this is my mum.

Read the words.

Notes for teachers
Target: To read these high frequency NLS words: and, I, like, me, school, they, you
This sheet can be used to record each child's progress. As a child successfully reads each word s/he can colour it on the sheet. You may like to take the opportunity to encourage the child to create a simple phrase or sentence using some of the words on the sheet. Write the child's sentence down so that s/he can copy it. Encourage careful writing and well formed letters.

Read the words.

and	I	like
me	school	they
	you	

and	I	like
me	school	they
	you	

Notes for teachers
Target: To read these high frequency NLS words: and, I, like, me, school, they, you
The children should cut out both sets of words and use them for making pairs, playing snap and matching to the 'school'
words on Worksheet 5. Can the children sequence the word cards to make the following phrases? I like school, you like
school, they like school, I like you, you like me, they like me and you.

Andrew Brodie: Supporting Literacy © A & C Black Publishers Ltd. 2006

Name: **Date:**

Read the words.

to   going   he

mum

she

the   was

Notes for teachers

Target: To read these YR high frequency NLS words: going, he, mum, she, the, to, was

This sheet can be used to record each child's progress. As a child successfully reads each word s/he can colour it on the sheet. You may like to take the opportunity to encourage the child to create a simple phrase or sentence using some of the words on the sheet. Write the child's sentence down so that s/he can copy it. Encourage careful writing and well formed letters.

Read the words.

going	he	she
the	mum	was
	to	

going	he	she
the	mum	was
	to	

Notes for teachers
Target: To read these YR high frequency NLS words: going, he, mum, she, the, to, was
The children should cut out both sets of words and use them for making pairs, playing snap and matching to the 'clown' words on Worksheet 7. Can the children make any phrases using the word cards? The following are possible: mum was going, he was going, she was going.

Name: _____

Date: _____

Read the words.

play

away

I

come

go

to

you

went

Notes for teachers

Target: To read these YR high frequency NLS words: away, come, go, I, play, to, went, you

This sheet can be used to record each child's progress. As a child successfully reads each word s/he can colour it on the sheet. You may like to take the opportunity to encourage the child to create a simple phrase or sentence using some of the words on the sheet. Write the child's sentence down so that s/he can copy it. Encourage careful writing and well formed letters.

Read the words.

away	come	go
I	play	to
went	you	

away	come	go
I	play	to
went	you	

Notes for teachers
Target: To read these YR high frequency NLS words: away, come, go, I, play, to, went, you
The children should cut out both sets of words and use them for making pairs, playing snap and matching to the 'dog' words on Worksheet 9. Can the children sequence the word cards to make the following phrases? I go away, you go away, I went away, you went away, I went to play, I go to play, you went to play, you go to play.

Andrew Brodie: Supporting Literacy © A & C Black Publishers Ltd. 2006

Name: _____ **Date:** _____

Read the words.

Notes for teachers
Target: To read these high frequency NLS words: am, are, in, I, he, is, school, she, you
This sheet can be used to record each child's progress. As a child successfully reads each word s/he can colour it on the sheet. You may like to take the opportunity to encourage the child to create a simple phrase or sentence using some of the words on the sheet. Write the child's sentence down so that s/he can copy it. Encourage careful writing and well formed letters.

Andrew Brodie: Supporting Literacy © A & C Black Publishers Ltd. 2006

Name: **Date:**

Read the words.

am	are	he
I	in	is
she	you	school

am	are	he
I	in	is
she	you	school

Notes for teachers

Target: To read these high frequency NLS words: am, are, at, are, he, I, in, is, school, she, you
The children should cut out both sets of words and use them for making pairs, playing snap and matching to the 'tractor' words on Worksheet 11. Can the children sequence the word cards to make the following phrases? I am in school, you are in school, she is in school, he is in school.

Name: _____   **Date:** _____

Read the words.

I   said   they

yes   dad

you

no

Notes for teachers
Target: To read these NLS high frequency words: dad, I, no, said, they, yes, you
This sheet can be used to record each child's progress. As a child successfully reads each word s/he can colour it on the sheet. You may like to take the opportunity to encourage the child to create a simple phrase or sentence using some of the words on the sheet. Write the child's sentence down so that s/he can copy it. Encourage careful writing and well formed letters.

Andrew Brodie: Supporting Literacy © A & C Black Publishers Ltd. 2006

Read the words.

dad	no	I
yes	they	you
	said	

dad	no	I
yes	they	you
	said	

Notes for teachers
Target: To read these YR high frequency NLS words: dad, I, no, said, they, yes, you
The children should cut out both sets of words. They can then be used for: matching, playing snap, matching to the owl
words on worksheet 13, or sequencing to make the phrases: I said yes, I said no, dad said yes, dad said no, you said yes, you
said no, they said yes, they said no.

Name: _____   Date: _____

Read the words.

is

it

the

big   dad

mum

school

Notes for teachers

Target: To read these NLS high frequency words: big, dad, is, it, mum, school, the

This sheet can be used to record each child's progress. As a child successfully reads each word s/he can colour it on the sheet. You may like to take the opportunity to encourage the child to create a simple phrase or sentence using some of the words on the sheet. Write the child's sentence down so that s/he can copy it. Encourage careful writing and well formed letters.

Read the words.

big	dad	is
it	mum	school
	the	

big	dad	is
it	mum	school
	the	

Notes for teachers

Target: To read these NLS high frequency words: big, dad, is, it, mum, school, the

The children should cut out both sets of words. They can then be used for: matching, playing snap, matching to the 'tortoise' words on Worksheet 15 or sequencing to make the following phrases: the school is big, it is big, dad is big, mum is big.

Name: _____

Date: _____

Read the words.

they

we

up

all

you

look

I

down

Notes for teachers
Target: To read these NLS high frequency words: all, down, I, look, they, up, we, you
This sheet can be used to record each child's progress. As a child successfully reads each word s/he can colour it on the sheet. You may like to take the opportunity to encourage the child to create a simple phrase or sentence using some of the words on the sheet. Write the child's sentence down so that s/he can copy it. Encourage careful writing and well formed letters.

Name: _____ **Date:** _____

Read the words.

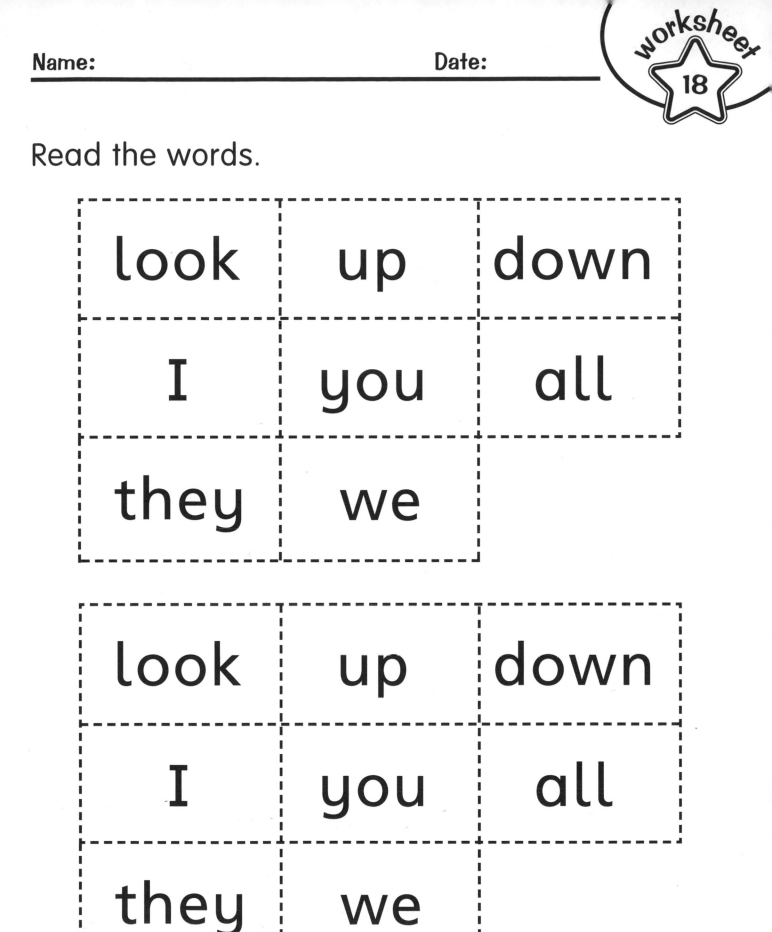

look	up	down
I	you	all
they	we	

look	up	down
I	you	all
they	we	

Notes for teachers:
Target: To read these NLS high frequency words: all, down, I, look, they, up, we, you
The child should cut out both sets of words. They can then be used for: matching, playing snap, matching to the 'fish' words on Worksheet 17, sequencing to make the phrases: I look up, I look down, you look up, you look down, they look up, they look down, we all look up, we all look down.

Read the words.

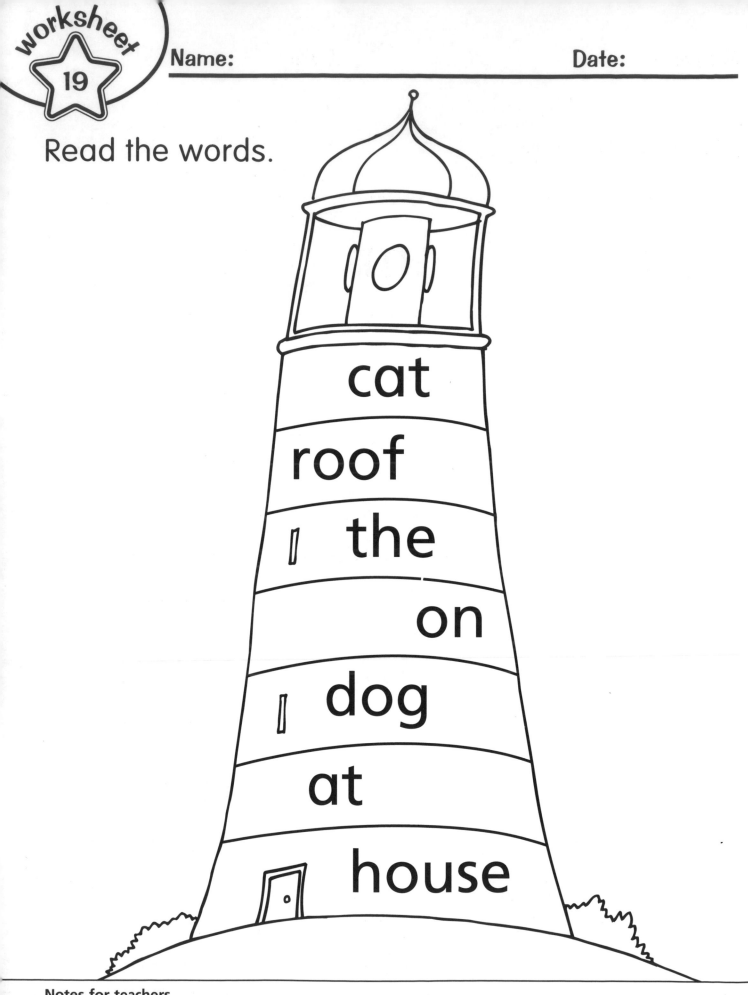

cat

roof

the

on

dog

at

house

Notes for teachers
Target: To read these NLS high frequency words: cat, dog, house, at, on, roof, the
This sheet can be used to record each child's progress. As a child successfully reads each word s/he can colour it on the sheet. You may like to take the opportunity to encourage the child to create a simple phrase or sentence using some of the words on the sheet. Write the child's sentence down so that s/he can copy it. Encourage careful writing and well formed letters.

Read the words.

at	cat	dog
house	is	on
roof	the	in

at	cat	dog
house	is	on
roof	the	in

Notes for teachers
Target: To read these NLS high frequency words: at, cat, dog, house, in, is, on, roof, the
The child should cut out both sets of words. They can then be used for: matching, playing snap, matching to the lighthouse words on Worksheet 19, sequencing to make the phrases: the dog is on the roof, the cat is on the roof, the dog is in the house, the cat is in the house.

Name:

Date:

Read the words.

bus

in

a

I

on

get

Notes for teachers
Target: To read these NLS high frequency words: a, bus, get, I, in, on
This sheet can be used to record each child's progress. As a child successfully reads each word s/he can colour it on the sheet. You may like to take the opportunity to encourage the child to create a simple phrase or sentence using some of the words on the sheet. Write the child's sentence down so that s/he can copy it. Encourage careful writing and well formed letters.

Read the words.

get	bus	I
in	a	on

get	bus	I
in	a	on

Notes for teachers
Target: To read these NLS high frequency words: a, bus, get, I, in, on
The child should cut out both sets of words. They can then be used for: matching, playing snap, matching to the 'bus' words on Worksheet 21, sequencing to make the phrase: I get on a bus.

Name: _____   **Date:** _____

Read the words.

Notes for teachers
Target: To read these NLS high frequency words: a, day, for, go, I, they, out, we
This sheet can be used to record each child's progress. As a child successfully reads each word s/he can colour it on the sheet. You may like to take the opportunity to encourage the child to create a simple phrase or sentence using some of the words on the sheet. Write the child's sentence down so that s/he can copy it. Encourage careful writing and well formed letters.

Read the words.

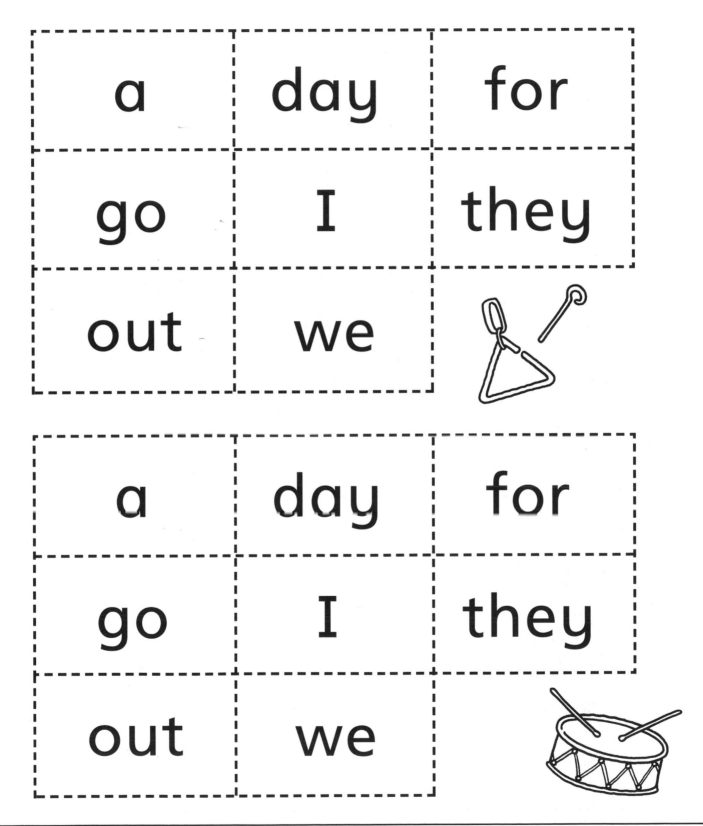

a	day	for
go	I	they
out	we	

a	day	for
go	I	they
out	we	

Name: _____   **Date:** _____

Read the words.

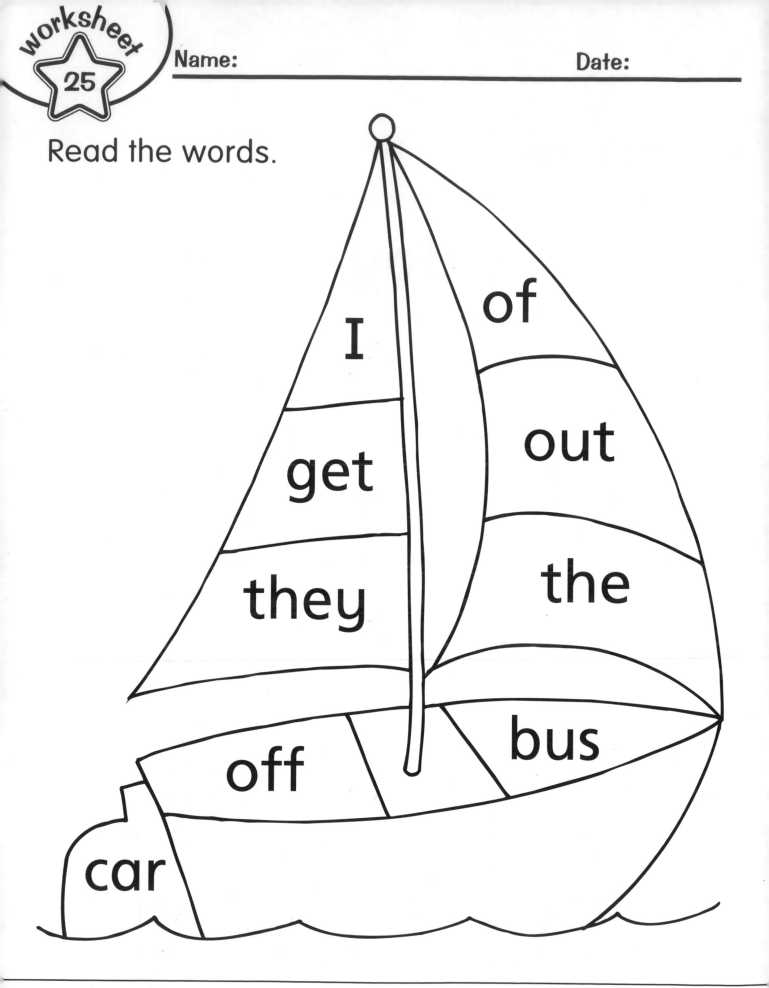

Name: _____ **Date:** _____

Read the words.

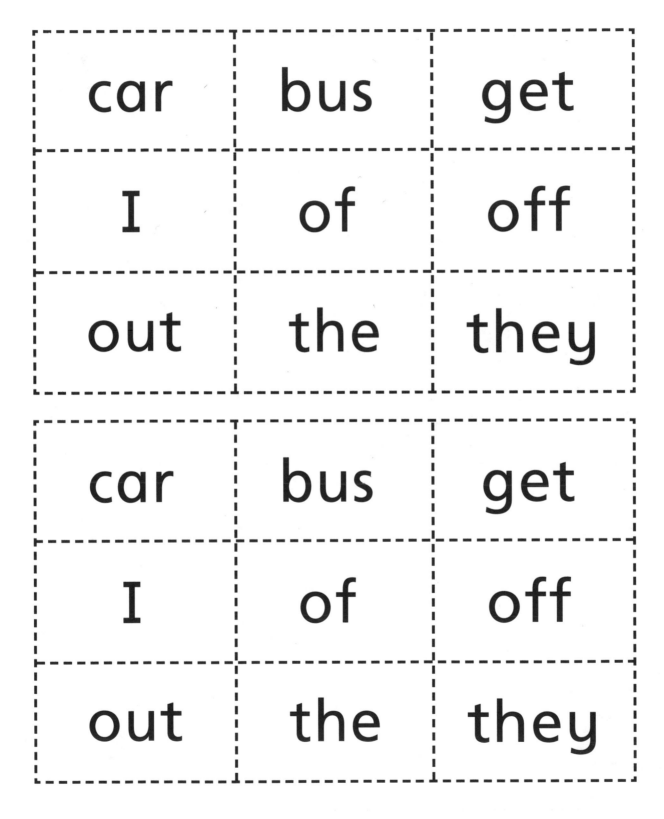

car	bus	get
I	of	off
out	the	they

car	bus	get
I	of	off
out	the	they

Notes for teachers
Target: To read these NLS high frequency words: car, bus, get, I, of, off, out, the, they
The child should cut out both sets of words. They can then be used for: matching, playing snap, matching to the 'yacht' words on Worksheet 25, sequencing to make the phrases: I get off the bus, they get off the bus, I get out of the car, they get out of the car.

Name: _____ **Date:** _____

Can you put the letters in the right order?

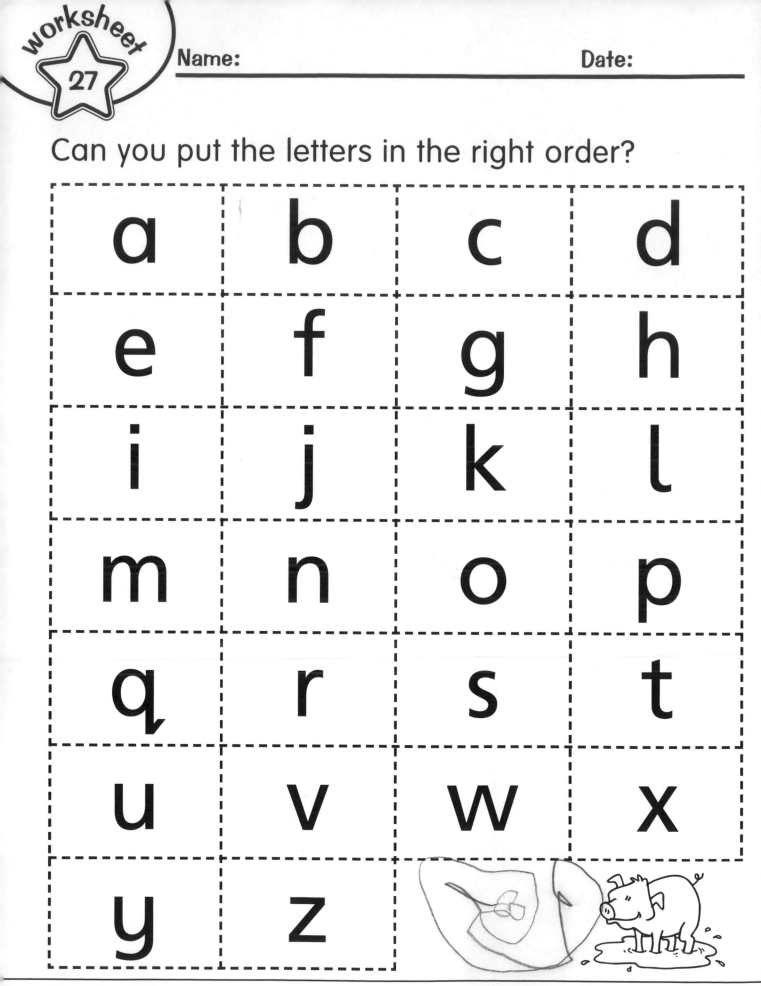

a	b	c	d
e	f	g	h
i	j	k	l
m	n	o	p
q	r	s	t
u	v	w	x
y	z		

Notes for teachers

Target: To learn the letters of the alphabet in order

The sheet should be photocopied twice. One copy can be cut into individual letters – ideally it should be laminated first. The individual letters should be presented to the child in random order to be placed on the complete sheet in the correct order, systematically starting from the letter a. Plastic letters could be used instead as many children find the tactile experience helpful.

Andrew Brodie: Supporting Literacy © A & C Black Publishers Ltd. 2006

Make the bed with your hands!

Notes for teachers:

Target: To correct b/d confusion

These ideas are useful for correcting b/d confusion. The child should practise saying 'bed' very clearly, stressing the b and the d sounds. They can learn to use their left hand to show the letter b and their right hand to show d.

Name: _____   Date: _____

Match the words beginning with **p**.

-------------------------   -------------------------

-------------------------   -------------------------   -------------------------

---

Notes for teachers:

Target: To identify initial letter sounds

This sheet should be used with the words from Resource sheet H (page 63). You may decide not to provide all of the words but just to select the words that begin with **p**. The child can then sort these by first finding those that match the pictures, then finding the other words in the 'p set'. Support them in writing the three words below the appropriate pictures, then in writing the other words on the other writing lines. It is important that the child has plenty of opportunities to read the words repeatedly. If you feel that the child is quite capable you could also supply him/her with some of the other words, for example the words beginning with **l**. They may notice that some of these words end with **p**.

Match the words beginning with **m**.

Notes for teachers
Target: To identify initial letter sounds
This sheet should be used with the words from Resource sheet H (page 63). You may decide not to provide all of the words just to select those that begin with **m**. The child can then sort them by first finding the words that match the pictures then finding the other words in the 'm' set. Support him/her in writing the three words below the appropriate pictures, then in writing the other words on the other writing lines. It is important that the child has plenty of opportunities to read the words repeatedly. If you feel that the child is quite capable you could also supply him/her with some of the other words, for example the words beginning with **n**. The letters **m** and **n** are similar in shape and structure; it is a good idea to stress the letter names and the sound that each makes, using some of the words to help to distinguish these, speaking very clearly and encouraging the child to repeat them clearly.

Name: _____   Date: _____

Match the words beginning with **b**.

-          -

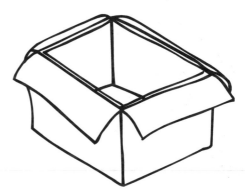

-          -

-          -

- - - - - - - - - - - - - -   - - - - - - - - - - - - - - - - -   - - - - - - - - - - - - - - - -

Notes for teachers

Target: To identify initial letter sounds

Use this sheet with the words from Resource sheet G (page 62). You may decide not to supply all of the words but just to select those that begin with **b**. The child can then sort these by first finding the words that match the pictures then finding the other words in the 'b set'. Support him/her in writing the four words below the appropriate pictures, then in writing the other words on the other writing lines. It is important that the child has plenty of opportunities to read the words repeatedly. If you feel that the child is quite capable you could also supply him/her with some of the other words, for example the words beginning with **d**. This would provide an opportunity to practise distinguishing between **b** and **d**.

Name: _____ **Date:** _____

Match the words ending with **d**.

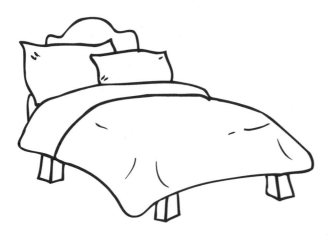

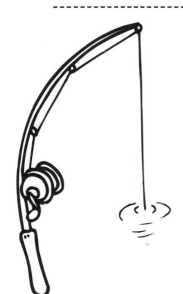

------------------------ ------------------------ ------------------------

------------------------ ------------------------

Notes for teachers

Target: To identify final letter sounds in consonant-vowel-consonant words

This sheet should be used with the words copied and cut out from Resource sheets G–I (page 62–64). You may decide not to supply all of the words but just to select the words that end with **d**. The child can then sort them by first finding those that match the pictures, then finding the other words that end with **d**. Support them in writing the four words below the appropriate pictures, then in writing the other words on the other writing lines. It is important that the child has plenty of opportunities to read the words repeatedly. If you feel that the child is quite capable you could also supply him/her with some of the other words, for example the words ending with **b**. This would provide an opportunity to practise distinguishing between **b** and **d**.

Name: _____   **Date:** _____

Find the words ending with **g**.

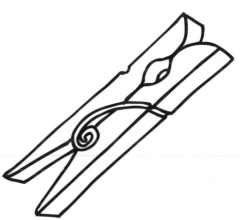

------------------------------   ------------------------------

------------------------------   ------------------------------

------------------------------   ------------------------------   ------------------------------

------------------------------   ------------------------------   ------------------------------

Notes for teachers

Target: To identify final letter sounds in consonant-vowel-consonant words

This sheet should be used with the words copied and cut out from Resource sheets G–I (pages 62–64). You may decide not to supply the words but just to select those that end with **g** (thirteen in total). You may decide not to use all of these or you could ask the child to read all of him/her but to choose only nine of them to write down, including those shown in the pictures. Support him/her in writing the four words below the appropriate pictures, then in writing the other words on the other writing lines. It is important that the child has plenty of opportunities to read the words repeatedly. If you feel that the child is quite capable you could also supply him/her with some of the other words, for example the words ending with **p**. This would provide an opportunity to practise reading both sets of words.

Name: _____   **Date:** _____

Find the words ending with **n**.

------------------------   ------------------------

------------------------   ------------------------

------------------------   ------------------------   ------------------------

------------------------   ------------------------   ------------------------

Notes for teachers

Target: To identify final letter sounds in consonant-vowel-consonant words

This sheet should be used with the words copied and cut out from Resource sheets G–I (pages 62–64). You may decide not to supply all of the words but just to select the words that end with **n** (ten words in total). You may decide not to use all of these or you could ask the child to read all of them but to choose only nine of them to write down, including those shown in the pictures. Support him/her in writing the four words below the appropriate pictures, then in writing the other words on the other writing lines. It is important that the child has plenty of opportunities to read the words repeatedly. If you feel that the child is quite capable you could also supply him/her with some of the other words, for example the words ending with **t**. This would provide an opportunity to practise reading both sets of words.

Name: _____ **Date:** _____

Funny Little House

Here is a cat
that wears a hat.

Here is a dog
and here is a frog.

Here is a louse
and here is a mouse.

They can all live together
in my funny little house.

Notes for teachers
Target: To identify rhyme and to find words that rhyme with those provided
Read the poem through to the child stressing the rhymes. You may need to read the poem two or three times before encouraging the child to join in with you. Then focus on the rhyming words, particularly cat/hat and dog/frog. Can the child think of other words that rhyme with these? Rhyming words for cat/hat: bat, mat, pat, rat, sat (Resource sheets G–I). Rhyming words for dog/frog: jog, log, hog. Ask the child to write these sets of rhyming words. This also provides an opportunity for you to discuss the initial consonant blend **fr**.

Tiny Little Flat

Here is a fish.
It is in a dish.

Here is a pig,
It has a wig.

Here is a cat
and here is a bat.

They can all live
together in my tiny little flat.

Notes for teachers

Target: To identify rhyme and to find words that rhyme with those provided
Read the poem through to the child stressing the rhymes. You may need to read the poem two or three times before
encouraging the child to join in with you. Then focus on the rhyming words, particularly pig/wig and cat/bat/flat. Can the
child think of other words that rhyme with these? Rhyming words for cat/bat/flat (Resource sheets G–I): hat, mat, pat, rat,
sat. Rhyming words for pig/wig: dig, rig. (Note that some children will be aware of the word rig as a term for a large truck;
it is also a term used in fishing, the name for the arrangement of ropes and sails on sailing ships, or an oil drilling platform!)
Ask the child to write these sets of rhyming words. This provides an opportunity for you to discuss the initial consonant
blend **fl** and the final **sh** sound.

Name: _____ **Date:** _____

Dad's Green Tent

Jon and Tam were going to play,

the sun was shining bright that day.

Out in the garden they both went

To try to put up their dad's green tent.

The poles went up, the poles fell down,

Jon and Tam began to frown.

They tried and tried and Tam felt sad,

So Jon went in to get their dad …

… and Dad did it!

Notes for teachers

Target: To identify rhyme and to find words that rhyme with those provided

Read the poem through to the child stressing the rhymes. You may need to read the poem two or three times before encouraging the child to join in with you. Then focus on the rhyming words, particularly play/day and sad/dad. Can the child think of other words that rhyme with these? Rhyming words for play/day include: way, away, say, may, pay, hay, ray, tray, clay, stay, today. Rhyming words for sad/dad: bad, had, lad, mad. Ask the child to write these sets of rhyming words. You can also consider the rhyming words went/tent where the letter e combines with the final consonant blend nt: bent, dent, rent, sent. The words down/frown have letter o combined with w to make the vowel consonant digraph ow: brown, crown. Look at the initial blends: **fr, br, cr.**

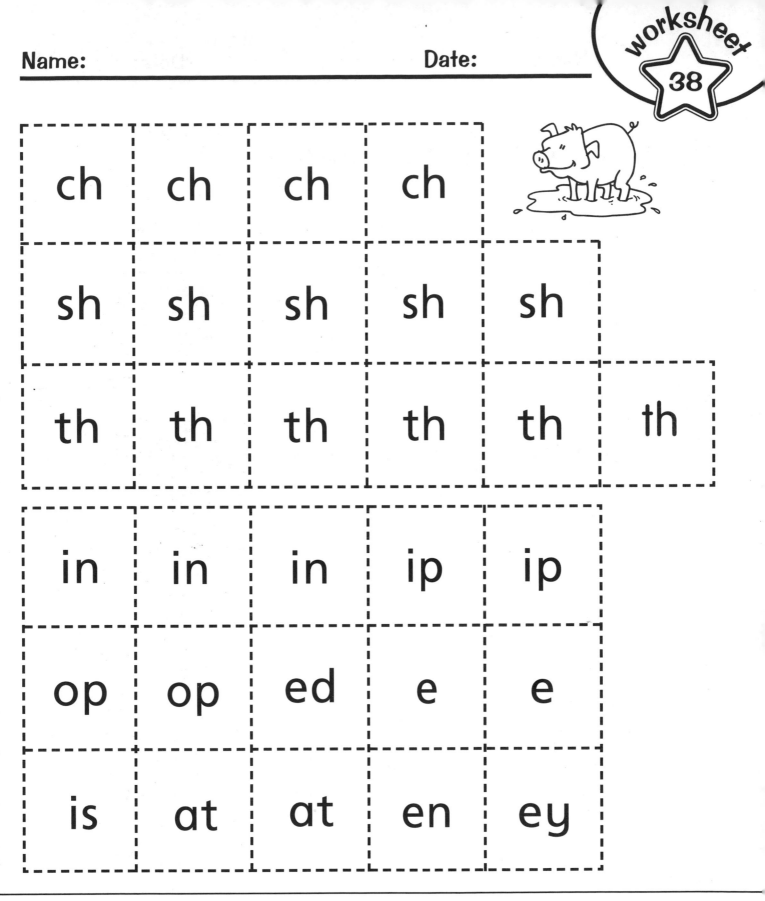

ch	ch	ch	ch	
sh	sh	sh	sh	sh
th	th	th	th	th	th
in	in	in	ip	ip
op	op	ed	e	e
is	at	at	en	ey

Notes for teachers

Target: To read words with initial sounds 'ch', 'sh' and 'th'

The sheet should be photocopied, laminated and cut into 'tiles'. This set of tiles gives the starts and ends of the following words:

chin	chip	chop	chat		
shin	ship	shop	shed	she	
thin	the	this	that	then	they

You could use the tiles in a game where the child has to create as many real words as possible. There are enough blends provided on the sheet to make all the words listed. If the child is able to do so, he/she could write the words down as they are discovered. Alternatively you may like to keep a large sheet of paper on the table so that you can write each word and discuss it as the child finds it – by the end of the lesson the sheet will be full of words that can be practised. Note that the word 'thin' has a different sound for th from the other words in the set.

Name:　　　　　　　　　　　**Date:**

Read the words. Write the words.

chin

chip

-------------------------　　　　　　　-------------------------

This is a chip.

Notes for teachers

Target: To read words with initial sound 'ch'

The sheet should be photocopied for use in discussion of the ch sound. You may like to remind pupils of combinations of blends that they have made using the tiles from Worksheet 38. Encourage them to read the words on this sheet, stressing the ch sound at the start of the words chin and chip. Ask them to copy the words, ensuring that they use the correct letter formation.

Read the words. Write the words.

ship

shed

She is a girl.

Notes for teachers:
Target: To read words with initial sound 'sh'
The sheet should be photocopied for use in discussion of the sh sound. You may like to remind pupils of combinations of blends that they have made using the tiles from Worksheet 38. Encourage them to read the words on this sheet, stressing the 'sh' sound at the start of the words ship, shed, shop and she. Ask them to copy the words, ensuring that they use the correct letter formation.

Andrew Brodie: Supporting Literacy © A & C Black Publishers Ltd. 2006

Name: **Date:**

Read the words	Write the words	Write and check
the		
they		
this		
that		
then		
thin		

They are thin.

Notes for teachers

Target: To read words with initial sound 'th'

The sheet should be photocopied for use in discussion of the 'th' sound. You may like to remind pupils of combinations of blends that they have made using the tiles from Worksheet 38. Encourage them to read the words on this sheet, stressing the 'th' sound at the start of the words the, they, this, that and then. Can they hear the different sound the 'th' makes in the word thin? Ask them to copy the words, ensuring that they use the correct letter formation.

Notes for teachers

Target: To sequence a set of four pictures identifying what each picture shows (Science 1, 2).
You may like to show the child the correct sequence of pictures and talk it through with him/her before cutting out the
pictures for the child to arrange in order. This activity can be extended by using Worksheet 43 where four sentences are
provided for the child to read with support and to put in the correct order.

Name: **Date:**

Cut out the sentences.

An egg is in a nest.

A chick comes out of the egg.

The chick grows bigger.

The chick grows into an adult.

Notes for teachers

Target: To sequence a set of four sentences to match the pictures on Worksheet 44
You may like to show the child the correct sequence of sentences and talk it through with him/her before cutting out the sentences to be arranged in order.

Notes for teachers

Target: To sequence a set of four pictures identifying what each picture shows (Science 1, 2)
You may like to show the child the correct sequence of pictures and talk it through with him/her before cutting out the pictures to be arranged in order. (Please note that Worksheets 46 and 47 feature a boy growing to become a man.) This activity can be extended by using Worksheet 45 where four sentences are provided for the child to read with support and to put in the correct order.

Cut out the sentences.

This is a baby girl.

She grows into a child.

She grows into a teenager.

She grows into a woman.

Notes for teachers

Target: To sequence a set of four sentences to match the pictures on Worksheet 44 (Science 1, 2)
You may like to show the child the correct sequence of sentences and talk it through with him/her before cutting out the
sentences for the child to arrange order. These sentences are designed for use with the pictures on Worksheet 44.

Notes for teachers

Target: To sequence a set of four pictures identifying what each picture shows (Science 1, 2)
You may like to show the child the correct sequence of pictures and talk it through with him/her before cutting out the pictures for the child to arrange in order. This activity can be extended by using Worksheet 47 where four sentences are provided for the child to read with support and to put in the correct order.

Name: _____

Date: _____

Cut out the sentences.

This is a baby boy.

He grows into a child.

He grows into a teenager.

He grows into a man.

Notes for teachers
Target: To sequence a set of four sentences to match the pictures on Worksheet 46 (Science 1, 2)
You may like to show the child the correct sequence of sentences and talk it through with him/her before cutting out the sentences for the child to arrange in order. These sentences are designed for use with the pictures on Worksheet 46.

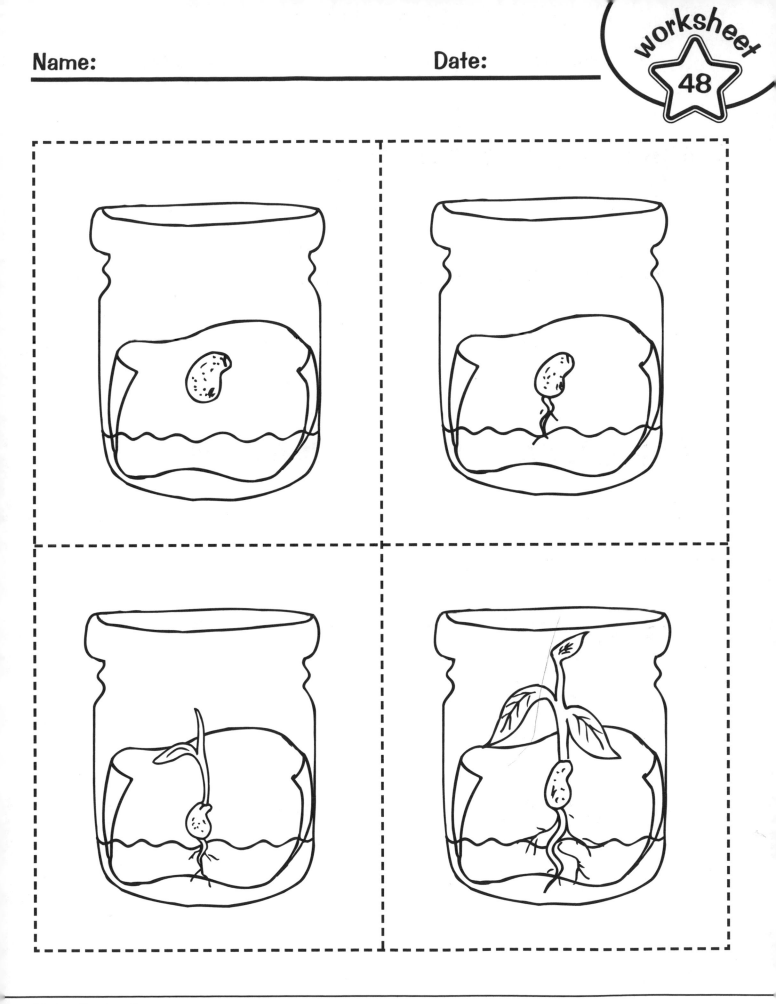

Notes for teachers

Target: To sequence a set of four pictures identifying what each picture shows (Science 1, 2)
You may like to show the child the correct sequence of pictures and talk it through with him/her before cutting out the pictures for the child to arrange in order. This activity can be extended by using Worksheet 49 where four sentences are provided for the child to read with support and to put in the correct order.

Name: _____   Date: _____

Cut out the sentences.

A bean seed in a jar with water.

The root begins to grow.

The shoot begins to grow.

The roots and shoot grow bigger.

Notes for teachers
Target: To sequence a set of four sentences to match the pictures on Worksheet 48 (Science 1, 2)
You may like to show the child the correct sequence of sentences and talk it through with him/her before cutting out the sentences for the child to arrange in order. These sentences are designed for use with the pictures on Worksheet 48.

Notes for teachers

Resource sheets A, B and C contain all the high frequency words recommended for Reception and can be used to create a useful set of flashcards for reading and spelling practice.

Resource sheets D, E and F provide some of the cvc words with visual clues and are designed to be copied, laminated if possible, then cut out as flashcards for matching activities.

Resource sheets G, H and I list a much larger collection of cvc words including and revising those featured on Resource sheets D, E and F. Again, if possible these should be copied and laminated before being cut out to create flashcards.

Some of the cards will be used with Worksheets 29, 30 and 31 where children are asked to find words beginning with p, m or b. In oral work you could also ask children to find words beginning with c, d, g, h, j, k, l, n, r, s, t, v, w or z.

Some of the cards will be used with Worksheets 32, 33 and 34 where children are asked to find words ending with d, g or n. You could also ask children to find words ending with b, m, p, s, t or x:

b: tub, web

d: bad, bed, did, had, lad, red, rod, sad, mud

g: bag, bug, dig, dog, hug, jug, leg, log, peg, pig, rig, tug, wag, zig-zag

m: him, jam, mum

n: bin, can, man, men, ran, sun, ten, tin, van, win

p: cap, cup, gap, hop, lap, mop, nap, nip, rap, rip, sip, tap, tip, top, zip

s: has, his, was

t: bat, bit, but, cat, cot, cut, fit, get, got, hat, hot, jet, kit, let, mat, net, not, pat, pet, pot, put, rat, sat, set, sit, wet

x: box, fox, six, wax

NLS High frequency words

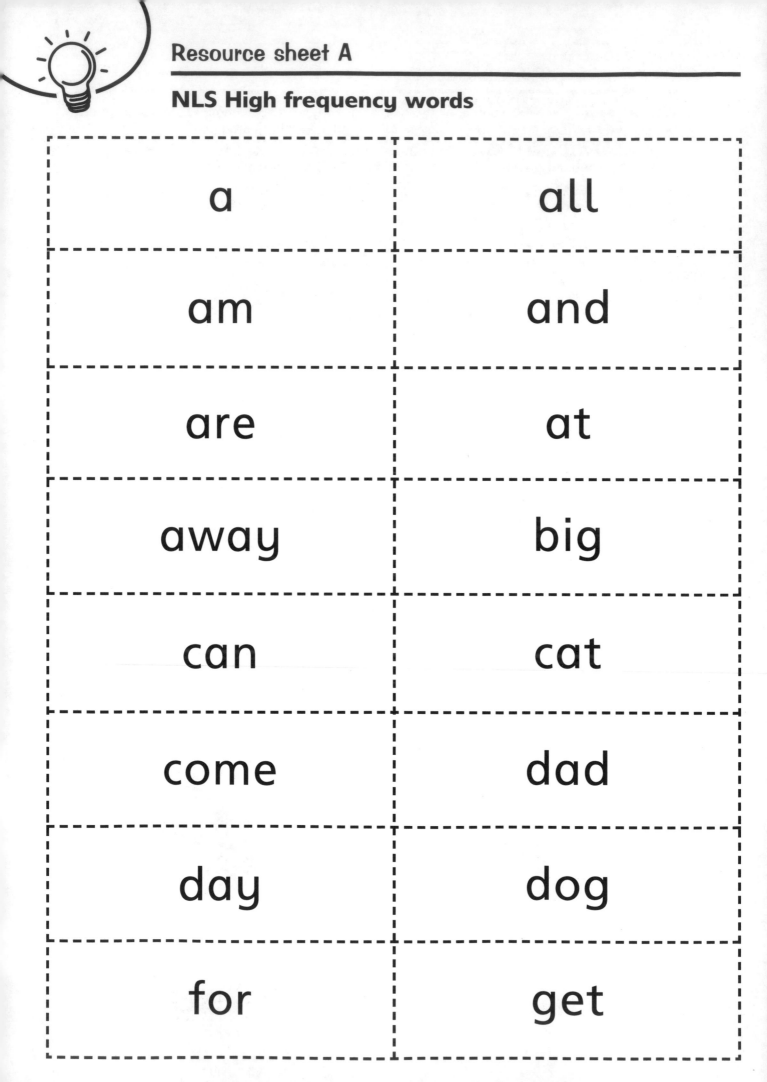

a	all
am	and
are	at
away	big
can	cat
come	dad
day	dog
for	get

NLS High frequency words

go	going
he	I
in	is
it	like
look	me
mum	my
no	of
on	play

NLS High frequency words

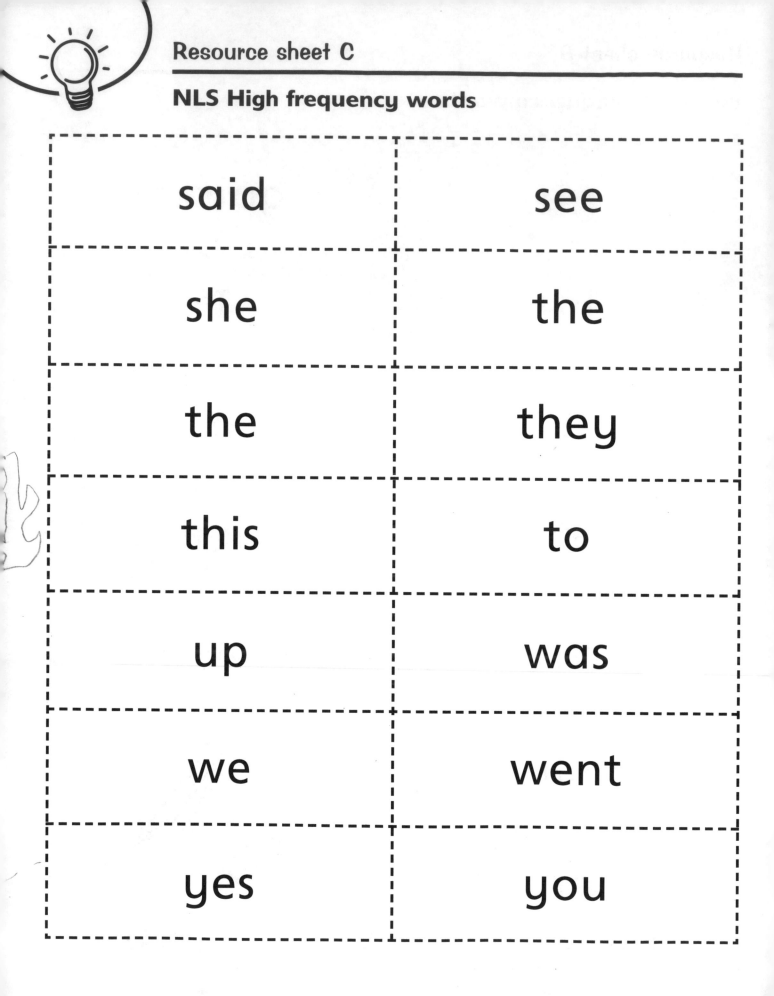

said	see
she	the
the	they
this	to
up	was
we	went
yes	you

cvc words with pictures

cat

dog

box

hat

jug

log

man

net

peg

Notes for teachers

This sheet should be copied then the individual 'tiles' should be cut out by an adult. Ideally the sheet should be laminated first. Alternatively, the sheet can be copied for the child to cut out the words if he/she has sufficient fine motor control to be able to use scissors effectively.

cvc words with pictures

rat

six

tap

ten

van

zip

bed

bag

cap

Notes for teachers

This sheet should be copied then the individual 'tiles' should be cut out by an adult. Ideally the sheet should be laminated first. Alternatively, the sheet can be copied for the child to cut out the tilif he/she has sufficient fine motor control to be able to use scissors effectively.

cvc words with pictures

cup   fox   jet

jam   leg   mop

pig   sun   web

Notes for teachers
This sheet should be copied then the individual 'tiles' should be cut out by an adult. Ideally the sheet should be laminated first. Alternatively, the sheet can be copied for the child to cut out the words if he/she has sufficient fine motor control to be able to use scissors effectively.

cvc words

box	bat	but
bit	bad	bag
bed	bin	bug
can	cap	cup
cut	cot	cat
dog	dig	did
dot	fox	fit
gap	gas	get
got	had	has
hat	his	him

Notes for teachers
This sheet should be copied, then the individual 'tiles' should be cut out - ideally the sheet should be laminated first.

cvc words

hot	hop	hug
jet	jog	jug
jam	kit	lip
leg	log	let
lap	lad	man
mat	mop	men
mum	mud	not
net	nip	nap
pig	pot	peg
pat	pet	put

Notes for teachers
This sheet should be copied, then the individual 'tiles' should be cut out - ideally the sheet should be laminated first.

cvc words

rat	rig	red
rap	ran	rip
rod	sad	sit
sat	set	sip
six	sun	tap
top	tip	ten
tin	tub	tug
van	wax	wag
was	wet	web
win	zip	zig-zag

Notes for teachers
This sheet should be copied, then the individual 'tiles' should be cut out - ideally the sheet should be laminated first.

Andrew Brodie: Supporting Literacy © A & C Black Publishers Ltd. 2006